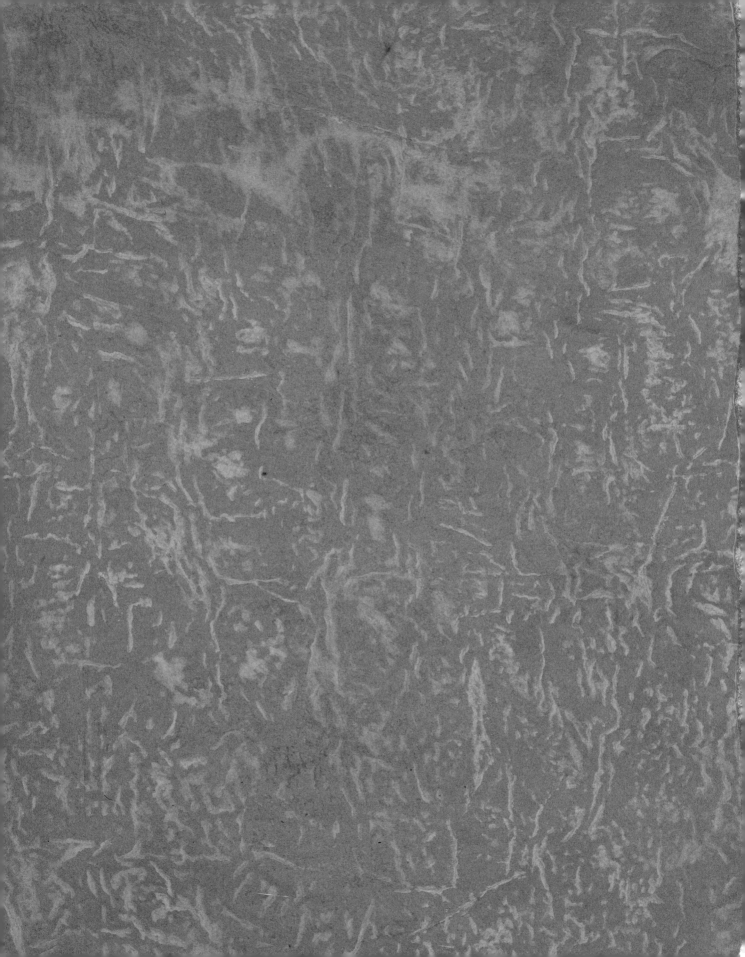

The FLAVORS of
PROVENCE

The FLAVORS of PROVENCE

PAINTINGS BY
Isabelle de Borchgrave

RECIPES AND TEXT BY
Jean-André Charial

RIZZOLI
NEW YORK

First published in the United States of America in 2004 by
Rizzoli International Publications, Inc.
300 Park Avenue South
New York, NY 10010
www.rizzoliusa.com

DESIGNER: Patricia Fabricant
PUBLISHER: Charles Miers
EDITOR: Christopher Steighner
TRANSLATOR: Anne de Ravel

2004 2005 2006 2007 / 10 9 8 7 6 5 4 3 2 1

Distributed in the U.S. trade by St. Martin's Press, New York

Printed in the USA

ISBN: 0-8478-2610-4

Library of Congress Catalog Control Number: 2003116892

Dedicated to my father,
a great cook, in memory

—ISABELLE DE BORCHGRAVE

CONTENTS

INTRODUCTION

For me, Provence is more a collection of sensations than a geographic region. It is impossible to illustrate in a book these sensations—for example, the lushness of Provence's fragrances. Instead, I have here tried to conjure up images that evoke particular moments from my memories.

My first encounter with the region came when, as a little girl, my parents took me to the Riviera on vacation. It was such a bright and sparkling place, worlds away from our native Brussels. One day on the beach our umbrella happened to be planted right next to that of Pablo Picasso! With the audacity that only a child can possess, I went right up and made friends with the great master. He invited me to his studio in Vallauris, and though I was too young to appreciate his art or the privilege, the memory of that visit stays with me to this day.

Many years later, as an adult with children of my own, I was again touched by the magic of Provence, but this time by the true Provence—the countryside. While traveling through the Luberon Mountain area, I became enchanted by the landscape of baked clay and blue skies and set out to capture this great melting pot of colors. I knew this was a place to which I had to return and paint again. My friend, the great painter of light, Pierre Lessieur, also spurred on my love of the region with his prolific studies of his house and garden in Saint-Remy de Provence. His work represents to me the essence of the entire Provençal landscape and is an enduring inspiration.

Each trip to Provence feeds my fascination, but it was one visit in particular that led to the creation of this book. Christian Tortu, the celebrated floral designer and a great friend of mine, guided me on a tour from Avignon to Camargue, through lavender and sunflower fields, roaming around markets and small towns to end up in the heart of the Alpilles Mountains. Just when my senses were at their most heightened, we came at last to Les Baux de Provence, where nature itself seems to pride itself on a pinch of austerity and touches of roughness.

Here in Les Baux, Tortu introduced me to Jean-André Charial, the proprietor of the picturesque Oustau de Baumanière hotel and restaurant. At the end of a delicious lunch, Charial told us this anecdote about himself: When a customer once inquired who had painted the picture hanging on one of the walls, Charial replied, "I am the artist. I have two passions—painting with oil and cooking with butter."

Charial and I then rambled through his garden as he picked the fresh peas of the day and described the herbs and vegetables with charming, old-fashioned names. I followed him in the midst of his chickens and lambs, the finishing touches in this classically Provençal scene. On that day, we decided we would celebrate the beauty of Provence by creating this book; I would hold the brush and he the whisk! We each contributed what we had absorbed of the region's essence. The result, I hope, will allow you to recreate in your own home some of the warmth and magic that is Provence.

—ISABELLE DE BORCHGRAVE

SOUPS

CREAM of RED PEPPER
SOUP with GINGER

ASPARAGUS VELOUTE
with OYSTERS

PROVENÇAL VEGETABLE
SOUP

TOMATO SOUP with BASIL

PISTACHIO VELOUTE with
SZECHUAN PEPPER

CURRIED
JERUSALEM
ARTICHOKE
VELOUTE

CREAMED ZUCCHINI
with SAFFRON

CREAM of RED PEPPER SOUP with GINGER

Crème de Poivrons Rouges au Gingembre

4 SERVINGS

½ pound red bell peppers, about 1 pepper
3 tablespoons unsalted butter
1 cup crème fraîche
3 cups chicken stock
½ teaspoon grated fresh ginger
Salt and freshly ground black pepper to taste

Halve the peppers, remove the seeds, and core. Cut into large pieces. Heat the butter in a saucepan over medium-high heat. Add the peppers and cook until they are softened and turn golden. Add the crème fraîche, chicken stock, and ginger. Lower the heat and simmer for 10 minutes.

Puree the mixture in a food processor or with a hand-held mixer. Return to the saucepan and reduce over low heat for 5 minutes. Strain the mixture, pressing down with a rubber spatula to obtain a fine creamy puree. Season with salt and pepper. This cream can be served as a soup or as a side dish with fish or shellfish.

ASPARAGUS VELOUTE with OYSTERS

Velouté d'Asperges aux Huitres

4 SERVINGS

1 large bunch green asparagus
2 tablespoons unsalted butter
2 cups fish stock
2 cups heavy cream
Salt and freshly ground black pepper to taste
1 dozen oysters

Trim and peel the asparagus stalks. Cut off the tips and set aside. Cut the asparagus stalks into ½-inch pieces. Blanch the asparagus tips in lightly salted water, until just tender. Drain and rinse under cold water to stop the cooking. Set aside.

Heat 1½ tablespoons of butter in a large heavy pot over medium heat. Add the asparagus stalks and cook for 4 to 5 minutes. Do not brown. Add the fish stock, cream, and salt. Simmer for 10 minutes. Puree the mixture in a food processor or blender and strain back into the pot.

Shuck the oysters over a strainer set over a small saucepan to collect the liquor. Gently warm the oysters in their liquor for just 1 minute, making sure not to overcook them. Remove with a slotted spoon and place three oysters at the bottom of four heated soup bowls. Heat the reserved asparagus tips in the remaining butter.

Stir the warm liquor into the velouté. Bring back to a simmer and adjust seasoning with salt and pepper. Ladle the warm velouté over the oysters and garnish with the asparagus tips.

PROVENÇAL VEGETABLE SOUP

Soupe au Pistou

4 TO 6 SERVINGS

SOUP:

1 pound fresh white shell beans or fresh cranberry beans, shelled (see note)

2 medium leeks, white and pale green parts only, thinly sliced

2 onions, thinly sliced

2 carrots, cut into small dice

1 pound potatoes, peeled and diced

1 BOUQUET GARNI: 1 bay leaf, 2 sprigs Italian parsley, 1 sprig thyme, 1 celery rib, wrapped in cheesecloth

½ pound green beans, trimmed and cut into ½-inch pieces

2 or 3 small zucchini, thinly sliced

¼ pound elbow macaroni

Salt and freshly ground black pepper to taste

PISTOU SAUCE:

1 very ripe medium tomato, peeled and diced

4 garlic cloves

2 cups packed basil leaves

1 cup extra virgin olive oil

Salt and freshly ground black pepper to taste

¾ cup grated Parmesan cheese

Bring 2½ quarts of salted water to a boil in a large pot. Add the beans, leeks, onions, carrots, potatoes, and bouquet garni. Bring back to a boil, cover, lower the heat to medium, and cook for about 30 minutes, or until the beans are very soft but hold their shape.

Add the green beans, zucchini, and macaroni. Cook for another 15 minutes, or until the macaroni is soft. Season with salt and pepper to taste.

Meanwhile, prepare the pistou sauce: Place the garlic, basil, 2 tablespoons of olive oil, salt, and pepper in a wood or marble mortar. Pound with the pestle until the mixture becomes a paste. Add a few tablespoons of the grated Parmesan and pound and stir until the mixture becomes firm. Add a third of the tomato and crush into the mixture. Continue pounding and mixing, alternating the cheese, tomato, and the olive oil. The mixture should be thick and unctuous. Set aside.

Remove the bouquet garni from the soup and serve hot with the pistou sauce on the side. Each diner can stir one or two spoonfuls of the mixture into the soup.

NOTE: If fresh beans are not available, use 1 cup of dry navy beans. Soak the beans overnight. Cook for 45 minutes or until tender. Drain. Proceed with the recipe.

SAVEURS DE PROVENCE: Tomatoes

Though it is a key ingredient in European cuisine, the tomato actually originated in the New World, where the Aztecs of Peru named it "tomatl." It was there that the Spanish conquistadors came upon a cherry-sized variety; they brought it back to Europe, where it was first planted only in gardens as an ornamental. Eventually though, the plant made its way up to the Mediterranean coastal regions, where it flourished.

It's hard to imagine Provençal cuisine without tomatoes. They are served raw in salads or in sandwiches, cooked in coulis and purees, dried in the oven or in the sun with olive oil, or preserved in pastes. They are indispensable in many classic recipes like ratatouille and gazpacho, and combinations of tomatoes with garlic, basil, and tarragon create enduring condiments.

To balance the tomato's acidity you can add sugar or cook it slowly to develop its own natural sugars. In this recipe, a Provençal version of gazpacho, I use honey for a floral effect.

TOMATO SOUP with BASIL

Soupe de Tomates au Basilic

4 SERVINGS

SOUP:

½ cup extra virgin olive oil

1 pound onions, thinly sliced

3 garlic cloves, minced

1 teaspoon honey

4 pounds very ripe tomatoes, quartered

Salt and freshly ground black pepper
to taste

1 bay leaf

2 sprigs thyme

¾ cup packed basil leaves

GARNISH:

1 small onion, finely diced

¼ cup coarsely chopped parsley
leaves

1 tomato, finely diced

2 tablespoons sherry vinegar

2 tablespoons extra virgin
olive oil

Heat 2 tablespoons of olive oil in a large pot over medium-low heat. Add the onion and garlic and cook until softened, about 5 minutes. Do not brown. Stir in the honey and cook until slightly caramelized. Add the tomatoes, salt, and pepper and cook, covered, for 40 minutes. Add the bay leaf, thyme, and basil and cook for another 10 minutes. Remove the bay leaf and thyme from the pot.

Puree the mixture in a food processor. Add the remaining olive oil and blend well. Strain the mixture into a bowl, pushing down to extract all the juices. Adjust the seasoning with salt and pepper and chill.

Combine all the ingredients for the garnish and marinate until ready to serve. Ladle the soup into chilled serving bowls and spoon some of the garnish on top.

2001

VE [afɛktif, iv] adj. –
ion, le cœur» bas lat.
e; touchant. 2. (1762)
ts de plaisir ou de
ions; ou complexes :
). ⇒ psychoaffectif.
tive : les sentiments,
ral. Réaction affective,
. (Extrait de Petit Robert)

PISTACHIO VELOUTE with SZECHUAN PEPPER

Velouté de Pistaches au Poivre de Sechuan

6 SERVINGS

1 pound pistachios, shelled and crushed
2 tablespoons honey
2 cups Champagne or good-quality sparkling wine
2 cups chicken stock
2 cups heavy cream
½ teaspoon ground Szechuan pepper
Juice of 1 lemon
Salt to taste

Set aside 6 tablespoons of pistachios for garnish. Place the honey in a medium saucepan set over high heat. Once the honey is liquid, add the pistachios at once and stir quickly to coat. Cook for 5 minutes until they start to caramelize.

Deglaze with the Champagne and simmer for 2 minutes. Add the chicken stock and cream and bring to a boil. Remove from heat. Puree the mixture using a food processor or a hand-held mixer. Return pot to the stove and simmer for 30 minutes.

Just before serving, strain the velouté through a fine sieve. Season with the Szechuan pepper, lemon juice, and salt. Garnish with the reserved crushed pistachios.

CURRIED JERUSALEM ARTICHOKE VELOUTE

Velouté de Topinambours au Curry

4 SERVINGS

1 pound Jerusalem artichokes
2 tablespoons extra virgin olive oil
1 teaspoon honey
1 teaspoon curry powder
2 cups chicken stock
1 cup light cream
Salt and freshly ground black pepper to taste

Wash and scrub the Jerusalem artichokes. Do not peel. Cut them into small dice.

Heat the olive oil in a large saucepan. Add the diced Jerusalem artichokes and sauté gently for 5 minutes. Stir in the honey to coat and continue to cook for a few minutes until they are slightly caramelized. Sprinkle with the curry powder.

Add the chicken stock and cream, and simmer for about 30 minutes. Pass the mixture through a fine-meshed strainer, pressing down with a rubber spatula to obtain a creamy soup. Season with salt and pepper. Serve immediately.

CREAMED ZUCCHINI
with SAFFRON

Crème de Courgettes
au Safran

6 SERVINGS

2 tablespoons extra virgin olive oil
1 small onion, sliced
2 pounds zucchini, sliced
½ teaspoon honey
Salt and freshly ground black pepper to taste
2 cups chicken stock
10 saffron threads
½ cup heavy cream
1 small bunch fresh mint

Heat the olive oil in a deep saucepan over medium heat. Add the onion and sauté until translucent. Add the zucchini and stir in the honey. Season with salt and pepper and let the mixture caramelize.

Add the chicken stock and saffron and simmer for 10 minutes. Stir in the cream and simmer for another 10 minutes. Remove from the heat, add the mint, and let infuse for 15 minutes. Discard the mint.

Puree the mixture in a food processor or with a hand-held mixer, and strain the mixture pressing down with a rubber spatula to obtain a fine creamy puree. Season with salt and pepper to taste. This dish can be served hot or cold.

APPETIZERS

TRUFFLE RAVIOLI with LEEKS

SARDINE TART

STUFFED ZUCCHINI BLOSSOMS

VEGETABLE MEDLEY with
FENNEL EMULSION

HEIRLOOM TOMATO TARTARE
INFUSED with SPICES

SWISS CHARD NAPOLEON with TRUFFLES

CRISP POTATO NAPOLEON
à la PROVENÇALE

TRUFFLE RAVIOLI with LEEKS

Ravioli de Truffe aux Poireaux

6 SERVINGS

RAVIOLI DOUGH:

3 eggs

1 tablespoon extra virgin olive oil

2½ cups flour

Pinch of salt

¾ pound sweetbreads

8 tablespoons unsalted butter

1 carrot, diced

1 small onion, diced

1 rib celery, diced

1 cup white wine

Salt and freshly ground black pepper to taste

4 leeks

1¾ ounces fresh black truffle

½ cup heavy cream

1 egg, beaten

¼ cup truffle juice

To make the ravioli dough: combine the eggs and olive oil in a small bowl. Heap the flour on a large wooden board and make a well in the center. Add the egg mixture and salt, using a fork to slowly incorporate them into the flour. When most of the mixture has been incorporated, start kneading using the palm of your hands. Continue kneading for 6 to 8 minutes, until the dough is soft and elastic. Dust with a little flour as you go along if the dough is too sticky. Wrap in plastic wrap and set aside at room temperature for 2 hours.

Rinse the sweetbreads under cold running water for 10 minutes. Bring some water to a boil in a small saucepan. Add the sweetbreads, simmer for 5 minutes, drain, and cool. Discard the outer membrane and connective tissues. Preheat the oven to 400 degrees.

Heat 2 tablespoons of butter over medium heat in an ovenproof skillet. Add the sweetbreads and diced vegetables, and sauté until golden. Add the white wine, season with salt and pepper, cover, and bake for 15 minutes. Remove from the oven and cool. When cool enough to handle, cut the sweetbreads into ½-inch cubes and reserve. Discard the vegetables.

Cut off the green part of the leeks and reserve. Thoroughly wash the white part and slice thinly. Combine 2 tablespoons of butter with 1 cup of lightly salted water in a saucepan. Add the sliced leeks and cook for 5 minutes or until tender. Drain and set aside. Cut about 1 ounce of the truffle into thin slices. Finely mince the remaining truffle and set aside.

To make the sauce, thoroughly wash the green part of the leeks and chop coarsely. Place in a saucepan with 2 cups of water, and simmer for 30 minutes. Puree the mixture in a food processor or with a hand-held mixer. Strain into a clean saucepan. Stir in the cream and remaining butter and reduce slightly over medium heat. Adjust seasoning to taste with salt and pepper.

Using a pasta machine set to the thinnest setting, roll out the dough. Cut into 2-inch squares. Brush the edges of the pasta squares with the beaten egg. Place a slice of truffle on each square. Top with a cube of sweetbread and a teaspoon of leeks. Cover with the remaining square and press around the edges to seal. Bring a large pot of salted water to a boil. Cook the ravioli for 5 minutes. Drain.

Meanwhile, reheat the leek sauce over medium heat and add the truffle juice. Add the ravioli to the sauce and simmer for few minutes to finish cooking. Spoon the ravioli into serving bowls and garnish with the reserved minced truffle.

SAVEURS DE PROVENCE: Olives

The olive tree is more than a plant—it is a symbol of happiness, peace, eternity, and fecundity. The climate of the Mediterranean region can be ideal for the olive tree, where it is known for the "liquid gold" it produces: olive oil. More than 2500 years ago, the Greeks brought the fabled tree to Provence, where its presence has brought a balance of success and failure. The tree can live for several centuries and harvests become increasingly generous as it ages. Frost is its worst enemy. Natives still remember the winter of 1956, when all the olive trees in Provence were lost.

Olives are gathered in the winter and processed into oil. Two types of oil are made here in the valley of Les Baux, France's premiere olive oil producing region. Oils with a prominent black flavor are made with lightly fermented olives and have aromas of vanilla and cooked artichokes. Oils with a green flavor come from olives pressed immediately and have a spicy, bitter taste of raw artichokes, almonds, fresh herbs, and peppery undertones.

SARDINE TART

2 tablespoons extra virgin olive oil
2 pounds onions, thinly sliced
3 anchovy fillets
1 teaspoon fresh thyme leaves

Freshly ground black pepper to taste
¾ pound store-bought puff pastry
¾ pound fresh sardines, boned and filleted
10 pitted black olives

Heat the olive oil in a large skillet over medium-low heat. Toss in the onions, anchovy fillets, and thyme. Cook for 40 minutes or until the onions are very soft. Adjust seasonings with pepper. Remove from the heat and refrigerate until the mixture is cold.

Preheat the oven to 425 degrees. Roll out the puff pastry into a rectangle about $1/8$-inch thick and place on a baking sheet. Spread with the cold onion mixture and arrange the sardine fillets and olives on top.

Bake for 20 minutes, until the pastry is puffed and golden. Remove from the oven and cool.

This tart can be served warm or cold, as an appetizer or main course with a tossed salad.

STUFFED ZUCCHINI BLOSSOMS

Fleurs de Courgettes Farcies

4 SERVINGS

STUFFING:
16 zucchini blossoms, zucchini attached
3 tablespoons extra virgin olive oil
⅓ cup diced Italian eggplant
20 pine nuts, toasted
¾ cup bread crumbs
¼ cup minced Italian parsley
1 small garlic clove, minced
3 tablespoons Parmesan cheese shavings
½ cup pitted black olives, minced
Salt and freshly ground black pepper to taste

BATTER:
¾ cup sifted flour
1 teaspoon baking powder
¾ cup beer, at room temperature
Peanut oil for frying

VINAIGRETTE:
1 tablespoon balsamic vinegar
Salt and freshly ground black pepper to taste
5 tablespoons virgin olive oil

The day before you plan on serving, prepare the blossoms. Cut off the zucchini of four zucchini blossoms and reserve. Open the four blossoms and discard the pistil. Place the flour for the batter in a bowl. Stir in the baking powder. Add the beer at once, stirring quickly to avoid any lumps. Set aside for 1 hour.

Heat the peanut oil at a depth of ¼ inch in a small skillet.
Spread the four reserved blossoms on a baking sheet. Coat one side evenly with the batter. Fry the blossoms on the battered side until golden. Arrange the blossoms on a clean baking sheet, then let them dry in an oven heated just to warm, or 140 degrees, for 2 hours. Turn the oven off and leave the flowers in the oven overnight without opening the door, to dry out completely.

To prepare the stuffing: cut the reserved 4 zucchini into thin slices. Heat the olive oil in a small skillet and sauté the diced eggplant and zucchini slices over medium-high heat until golden brown. Drain on paper towels.

Bring a large pot of lightly salted water to a boil. Blanch the remaining 12 zucchini blossoms with their attached zucchini for 2 minutes. Carefully remove with a slotted spoon and drain on paper towels.

Combine the eggplant, zucchini slices, pine nuts, bread crumbs, parsley, garlic, Parmesan, and black olives in a small bowl. Stir well to blend. Adjust seasoning to taste with salt and pepper. Spoon some of the mixture into the blanched blossoms, filling them about three-quarters full. Fold the tips of the blossoms over the stuffing. Refrigerate until ready to use.

When ready to serve, preheat the oven to 400 degrees. Prepare the vinaigrette by combining the balsamic vinegar with salt and pepper. Whisk in the olive oil. Arrange the stuffed blossoms and their zucchini in one layer in a baking dish. Bake for 10 to 12 minutes, just until heated through. Arrange the stuffed blossoms on serving plates and drizzle some of the vinaigrette over them. Garnish each plate with a crisp oven-dried blossom.

NOTE: Look for zucchini with blossoms attached from late spring to summer at your local farmer's market, or better yet, grow your own.

VEGETABLE MEDLEY with FENNEL EMULSION

Mélange de Legumes à l'Emulsion de Fenouil

4 SERVINGS

VEGETABLE MEDLEY:
Juice of half lemon
1 artichoke
1 pear
¼ cup extra virgin olive oil
1 peach, thinly sliced
1 zucchini, cut into large cubes
1 carrot, cut into large cubes
1 fig, quartered
1 large onion, sliced
2 yellow pattypan squash, quartered
2 green pattypan squash, quartered

2 asparagus, cut into 4-inch pieces
8 snow peas, trimmed
Salt and freshly ground black pepper to taste

FENNEL EMULSION:
¾ cup extra virgin olive oil
¼ cup rice vinegar
¼ cup pastis
½ teaspoon unflavored gelatin
Salt and freshly ground black pepper to taste
1 tablespoon minced wild fennel or fennel tops
4 ice cubes

Combine the lemon juice with 1 cup of cold water. Cut off the stem of the artichoke across the base. Break off the dark green leaves until the pale tender ones are exposed. Using a sharp paring knife, trim all around the base as closely as possible without cutting or shaving the heart. Cut crosswise, removing the top two-thirds of the leaves. Halve the artichoke heart and cut each half into eight wedges. Scrape out the center choke. Place the wedges in the lemon water as you go along to avoid discoloration. Peel and quarter the pear. Discard the center core and cut each quarter into 3 or 4 slices.

Place the olive oil in a large skillet over medium-low heat. Add all the vegetables and fruits, and season with salt and pepper. Toss well, and cook over medium heat, stirring once in a while, for 15 to 20 minutes, or until all the vegetables are cooked through.

Meanwhile, prepare the emulsion. Place half of the olive oil, the vinegar, pastis, gelatin, salt, pepper, fennel, and ice cubes in a blender. With the machine running, add the remaining olive oil in a slow stream. The mixture should be well emulsified and almost white. Strain into a bowl. To serve, pour some of the emulsion into the bottom of four shallow serving plates and spoon some vegetables over it.

HEIRLOOM TOMATO TARTARE INFUSED with SPICES

Petit Tartare de Tomates Anciennes Infusées aux Epices

6 SERVINGS

2 pounds assorted heirloom tomatoes such as Cherokee Purple, Brandywine, Green Zebra, Black Krim, etc., peeled (see note below)

8 plum tomatoes

2 tablespoons extra virgin olive oil

¼ cup toasted almond oil

5 mint leaves, chopped

2 vanilla beans, split lengthwise and coarsely chopped

Zest of 1 lemon

Zest of 1 lime

3 star anise

¾ cup fresh almonds or skinless blanched almonds, coarsely chopped

1 tablespoon maple syrup

½ cup packed purple basil

Salt and freshly ground black pepper to taste

Fleur de sel, preferably from Camargue

Basil-flavored olive oil for garnish

Balsamic vinegar for garnish

Parmesan shavings for garnish

12 celery leaves for garnish

Preheat the oven to 250 degrees. Halve the plum tomatoes lengthwise and discard the seeds. Place the plum tomato halves on a baking sheet and drizzle with the olive oil. Bake for 2 hours. Combine the toasted almond oil with the mint, vanilla beans, the lemon and lime zests, and the star anise. Set aside and marinate for 2 hours or until ready to use. Strain the oil and discard the spices.

Place the roasted plum tomatoes in the bowl of a food processor. Add ½ cup of the almonds, the maple syrup, and purple basil. Season to taste with salt and pepper and process to a coarse puree.

Halve the heirloom tomatoes lengthwise, discard the seeds, and cut into ¼-inch strips. Toss in the remaining almonds. Season with the fleur de sel and the strained infused almond oil. Spoon some of the tomato puree on individual serving plates. Drizzle a few drops of basil oil and balsamic vinegar around it. Top with the heirloom tomato tartare and garnish with a few shavings of Parmesan and the celery leaves.

NOTE: To peel red tomatoes, first bring a pot of water to a boil. Score the skins of the tomatoes with a sharp knife and plunge them in the water for 12 seconds. Remove and plunge them in cold water to stop the cooking. The skins should now slip off easily.

SAVEURS DE PROVENCE: Truffles

The truffle is a fascinating food with a unique perfume, conjuring up the stifling heat of humus. The taste creates pleasure in three steps: its aroma, its flavors on the palate, and the lingering aftertaste. The taste is simply intoxicating, both peppery and subtle.

Truffles are most often associated with Périgord in the south of France, yet 70 percent of black French truffles come from Provence. But no matter the region, truffles are extremely rare; truffle-hunting hounds and sows are used to track the elusive treasures, which can be hidden as deep as 2 feet deep underground. Everything in the truffle's appearance reflects its subterranean habitat, but its extraordinary flavor expresses a lightness and delicacy that are seldom associated with such earthy origins.

The truffle is a great match for game meats, fine fish, and some shellfish, but also for pasta or the humble potato. Its strong flavor does not overwhelm other ingredients; on the contrary, it underscores them. Truffles have an affection for wine. Choosing mature wines is best; the fruity and woody notes of younger wines are rarely a good companion for the complex taste of the truffle.

SWISS CHARD NAPOLEON with TRUFFLES

Millefeuille de Blettes aux Truffes

6 SERVINGS

1 small celery root, about 1 pound
1 cup milk
½ cup cream
Salt and freshly ground black pepper to taste
Juice of half lemon
6 large, unblemished Swiss chard leaves, stalks removed
3½ ounces fresh truffle
1½ cups chicken stock
2 tablespoons unsalted butter
¾ cup truffle juice

Peel the celery root and cut into small cubes. Combine the milk with 3 cups of salted water in a large saucepan and bring to a boil. Add the celery root and simmer until tender, about 15 minutes. Drain. Place in a food processor with the cream and puree until smooth. Adjust the seasoning with salt and pepper and set aside.

Bring a large pot of salted water to a boil. Add the lemon juice. Blanch the Swiss chard leaves for 2 minutes, just to soften them. Carefully remove from the pot, making sure not to tear them, and spread on paper towels to drain.

Slice about 2 ounces of the truffle and place in a small saucepan. Add 3 tablespoons of the chicken stock and "sweat" over very low heat for 15 minutes. Pour into the bowl of a food processor and process to a coarse puree. Preheat the oven to 275 degrees.

Cut the Swiss chard leaves into twelve 5-inch by 2½ -inch rectangles. Cut 1 ounce of the truffle into thin slices. Place six of the Swiss chard rectangles on a non-stick baking sheet. Spread the Swiss chard with the truffle puree. Cover with the celery root and top with a few slices of truffles. Cover with the remaining rectangles. Bake for 20 minutes.

Reduce the remaining chicken stock by one-quarter. Whisk in the butter. Add the truffle juice, season with salt and pepper, and emulsify using a hand held mixer or blender. To serve, julienne the remaining truffle. Spoon some of the sauce into serving plates and top with a napoleon. Garnish with the julienned truffle.

CRISP POTATO NAPOLEON
à la PROVENÇALE

Craquant de Pommes de Terre en Millefeuille, Tomate Confite, Artichauts, Saveur Provençale

4 SERVINGS

4 plum tomatoes, peeled (see note, page 36)

3 tablespoons olive oil

8 small purple artichokes

8 pitted Taggiasche or Niçoise olives, halved

¼ cup minced Italian parsley

4 scallions, thinly sliced

Salt and freshly ground pepper to taste

2 to 3 large potatoes, Bintje or Yukon Gold

1 cup peanut oil

2 tablespoons veal stock, heated

Preheat the oven to 250 degrees. Halve the tomatoes lengthwise and discard the seeds. Place the tomato halves on a baking sheet and drizzle with 1 tablespoon of olive oil. Bake for 2 hours. Set aside.

Cut off the stems of the artichokes across the base. Break off the tough outer leaves until the pale tender ones are exposed. Using a sharp paring knife, trim all around the bases as closely as possible without cutting or shaving the hearts. Cut crosswise, removing the top two-thirds of the leaves. Halve the artichoke hearts. Scrape out the center chokes.

Heat the remaining 2 tablespoons of olive oil in a large skillet. Sauté the artichokes over medium-high heat for 10 minutes, until cooked through and golden brown. Stir in the olives, parsley, scallions, and confit tomatoes. Season with salt and pepper.

Peel the potatoes and cut them lengthwise into ¼-inch slices. You should have sixteen large, uniform slices. Heat the peanut oil in a large skillet over medium-high heat. Add the potato slices in one layer and fry until golden on both sides and crisp. Drain on paper towels. Repeat with the remaining potato slices. Sprinkle the crisp potato slices with salt.

To serve, place a crisp potato slice at the center of four serving plates. Spread with some of the artichoke mixture and top with a potato slice. Repeat the layers with the remaining artichokes and potatoes. Drizzle some veal stock around the napoleon and serve immediately.

FISH

RED MULLET with BASIL

STRIPED BASS with PROVENÇAL
RED WINE SAUCE

STEAMED JOHN DORY with
MANDARIN-FLAVORED OLIVE OIL

SEA BASS with SAFFRON
VINAIGRETTE

SAUTEED LOBSTER with SPICES

ROASTED TURBOT with
LIME SAUCE

TUNA STEAK with FRESH HERBS
and CLAMS

SAVEURS DE PROVENCE: Basil

Beyond its culinary uses, basil appears in religious traditions around the world. In ancient Persia, basil was so sacred that only the king was allowed to pick it. In India it is called holy basil, and its Greek name basilikon means "royal."

Basil types range in color from green to purple. Its amazing genetic variety is what has allowed it to adapt to so many different environments. It grows easily in warm, humid climates and loves to have its head in the hot sun and its feet in the cool earth. Thus it thrives in Provence and has become a cornerstone of Provençal cuisine. The sound of crickets chirping, the scent of basil and other herbes de Provence—these perfectly conjure up the warmth of the region.

Basil works well in any dish that includes tomatoes, vegetables, or fish. The best-known Provençal basil-based preparation is pistou, meaning "crushed in Provence." It is made by crushing garlic, salt, and basil leaves in a bowl while slowly adding olive oil. If you add grated Parmesan and pine nuts, you have Italian pesto.

RED MULLET with BASIL
Rougets au Basilic

4 SERVINGS

4 medium tomatoes, peeled (see note, page 36)
½ cup minced basil plus 1 tablespoon for garnish
1¼ cups extra virgin olive oil, preferably from Provence
1 tablespoon sherry vinegar
Salt and freshly ground black pepper to taste
8 red mullets, about 3½ ounces each, scaled, cleaned, and filleted

Prepare the sauce a day or two before you plan to serve the dish: Halve the tomatoes crosswise and discard the seeds and core. Cut the tomatoes into small dice. Place the tomatoes, ½ cup basil, 1 cup olive oil, and vinegar in a bowl and stir to combine. Season to taste with salt and pepper and refrigerate until ready to use.

To prepare the final dish, divide the remaining 4 tablespoons of olive oil between two large nonstick skillets. Heat the oil over medium heat. Season the mullet fillets with salt and pepper on both sides and place them skin side down in the skillets. Cook for 2 minutes. Turn the fillets and cook for 2 to 3 minutes longer.

To serve, spoon some marinated tomatoes in the center of individual serving plates. Top with four mullet fillets and drizzle with the sauce. Garnish with basil. Serve immediately.

STRIPED BASS with PROVENÇAL RED WINE SAUCE

Loup au Vin Rouge des Baux

6 SERVINGS

¼ pound fish bones, preferably from lean white fish

10 tablespoons unsalted butter

1 leek, white part only, thinly sliced

1 small onion, thinly sliced

2 shallots, thinly sliced

1 garlic clove, thinly sliced

1 bottle good red wine, preferably from Provence

4 small tomatoes, peeled, halved, and seeded (see note, page 36)

6 tablespoons olive oil

¾ cup black olives, pitted

½ bunch of chives, thinly sliced

Salt and freshly ground black pepper to taste

¼ cup Italian parsley leaves, chopped

6 striped bass fillets, about 4 ounces each, with the skin on

Preheat the oven to 375 degrees. Roast the fish bones for 15 minutes, until slightly golden. Remove. Lower the temperature to 250 degrees.

Heat 1 tablespoon of butter in a large saucepan over medium-low heat. Add the leek, onion, shallots, and garlic. Stir well, cover, and cook gently for 4 to 5 minutes, until the vegetables soften. Add the roasted fish bones and the wine. Bring to a boil; lower the heat to a simmer and cook uncovered for 1 hour or until the wine has reduced to about ⅓ cup. Strain through a fine sieve, discard the solids, and reserve the wine reduction.

Meanwhile, place the tomato halves on a baking sheet, drizzle with 3 tablespoons olive oil, and roast for 2 hours, until soft and slightly

46

caramelized. Set aside to cool and cut into small dice.

When ready to serve, preheat the oven to 400 degrees. Heat 1 tablespoon butter in a skillet, and sauté the diced tomatoes, olives, and chives, until warm. Adjust seasoning with salt and pepper and toss in the parsley. Keep warm.

Slowly reheat the wine reduction. When it is warm but not boiling, remove from the heat and whisk in the remaining butter, a few pieces at a time, until the sauce is smooth and emulsified. Adjust seasoning with salt and pepper and keep warm.

Heat the remaining olive oil in a large ovenproof skillet. Season the bass fillets on both side with salt and pepper. Place in the skillet skin-side down, and cook over medium heat for 3 to 4 minutes. Place the skillet in the oven and cook for 4 to 5 minutes or according to taste.

Arrange the bass fillets on serving plates. Scatter the tomato mixture around and spoon the sauce over the fish.

OU CÈU D'AZUR DE LA BELLO PROUVÈNÇO
DE LAMANOUN IS ÈR TANT AGRADIÈN :
ASTRE D'AMOUR, LI PÈRLO DE JOUVÈNÇO
BORD D'OU CAMIN, CANTAS EN PLEIN ESTIÈU.
(G. VASSEL).

2 — Arlésienne

EN PROVENCE. — Type d'Arlésienne

29 EN PROVENCE. — Arléstennes. — LL

STEAMED JOHN DORY with MANDARIN-FLAVORED OLIVE OIL

Saint Pierre Vapeur à l'Huile d'Olive Mandarine

4 SERVINGS

1 small spaghetti squash
2 tablespoons extra virgin olive oil
Salt and freshly ground black pepper to taste
3 tablespoon minced Italian parsley
2 whole John Dory or porgy, about 1¾ pounds each, scaled, cleaned, and filleted
2 tablespoons mandarin-flavored olive oil from O & Co. (see note)

Halve the spaghetti squash lengthwise and remove the seeds. Place the squash in the top part of a steamer set over salted boiling water. Steam for 20 to 30 minutes or until soft. Remove from the steamer and cool.

When cool enough to handle, run the tines of a fork through the flesh and separate into spaghetti-like strands. Heat the olive oil in a skillet over medium heat. Add the spaghetti squash and sauté for a few minutes, until hot. Season with salt and pepper and sprinkle with the minced parsley. Keep warm.

Season the fish fillets with salt and place in the top part of a steamer set over boiling water. Steam for 3 minutes, or until just cooked.

Arrange some of the spaghetti squash in the center of each serving plate. Top with a steamed fillet of fish. Season with freshly ground pepper and drizzle with the mandarin-flavored oil.

NOTE: Mandarin-flavored olive oil is a specialty olive oil from O & Co. The olives and mandarins are pressed together to create an oil with a distinct orange flavor. To purchase the mandarin-flavored oil or find out about retail stores, log onto www.oliviersandco.com.

SEA BASS with SAFFRON VINAIGRETTE

Daurade à la Vinaigrette Safranée

4 SERVINGS

8 stalks asparagus
2 carrots, cut into 1-inch dice
2 small zucchini, cut into 1-inch dice
1 small fennel bulb, thinly sliced
2 young leeks, cut into 1-inch pieces
2 tablespoons unsalted butter
8 cherry tomatoes
Salt and freshly ground black pepper to taste
4 sea bass fillets with their skin,
about 5 ounces each
2 tablespoons olive oil

SAFFRON VINAIGRETTE:
Juice of half lemon
3 leaves lemon verbena, minced
30 saffron threads (about 1 teaspoon)
2 tablespoons soyu (see note)
3 tablespoons cider vinegar
½ cup olive oil

The day before you plan on serving, whisk all the ingredients for the saffron vinaigrette in a small bowl. Cover and refrigerate.

Peel and trim the asparagus, discarding the tough part of the stalks. Cut the tips into 1-inch pieces. Bring a large saucepan of salted water to a boil. Fill a large bowl with cold water and ice cubes. Blanch the asparagus, carrots, zucchini, fennel, and leeks separately for a few minutes each in the boiling water, until cooked but still crisp. Remove from the pot and plunge in the ice bath to stop the cooking. Drain. Heat the butter in a skillet over medium heat. Sauté the blanched vegetables and tomatoes until warm. Adjust seasoning to taste with salt and pepper.

Score the skin of the sea bass fillets with a sharp knife. Season with salt and pepper on both sides. Heat the olive oil in a large skillet over medium-high heat. Place the fillets skin side down and cook for 3 minutes. Turn the fillets and cook for 2 to 3 minutes, or until done to taste. Place the fish fillets in the center of serving plates. Arrange the vegetables around them and drizzle with the saffron vinaigrette.

NOTE: Soyu is a Japanese soy sauce that is naturally fermented and lower in sodium than the Chinese sauce.

SAUTEED LOBSTER with SPICES

Homard Bleu Sauté à Cru aux Epices

4 SERVINGS

8 tablespoons butter, clarified (see note below)

2 tablespoons unsalted butter

2 garlic cloves

4 lobsters, about 1¼ pounds each

4 shallots, chopped

3 carrots, diced

1 stalk celery, diced

½ cup Sauternes wine

1 small bunch basil, minced

3 cups chicken stock

¼ teaspoon curry powder

Fleur de sel

Basil-flavored extra virgin olive oil, preferably from Provence

Bring a small pot of water to a boil and blanch the garlic cloves for 4 minutes. Drain and set aside. Bring a large stockpot of water to a boil. Add the lobsters to the boiling water and cook for 2 minutes. Remove from the pot and drain. When cool enough to handle, separate the bodies from the tails. Remove the shells from the tails. Reserve the meat. Crack the claws and reserve the meat. Halve the bodies and discard any nonedible parts. Pound the shells into large pieces.

Heat half of the clarified butter in a large sauté pan over high heat. Add the crushed lobster shells and bodies and sauté until golden. Add the shallots, carrots, celery, and blanched garlic and cook, stirring, for 3 minutes. Deglaze with the Sauternes wine and reduce until it has almost evaporated. Stir in the basil and chicken stock, lower the heat to simmer, and cook for 30 minutes or until the liquid has reduced by half. Strain into a saucepan.

Place the saucepan over medium heat, add the curry powder, and whisk in the remaining 2 tablespoons of butter. The sauce should be homogenous and smooth. Keep warm.

Heat the remaining clarified butter in a skillet over medium-high heat. Add the lobster tail meat and cook for 2 minutes on each side. Add the claw meat and cook for 2 minutes longer. Remove from the heat and season with fleur de sel. Place the lobster tails and claws into shallow serving plates. Spoon the sauce over them and drizzle with basil-flavored olive oil.

NOTE: To make clarified butter: place the butter in a small saucepan. Melt over medium-low heat and cook until the foam disappears and the white milky residue settles at the bottom. Do not brown the butter. Strain the melted butter through a damp cheesecloth or paper towel into a clean bowl, discarding the milky residue left behind.

ROASTED TURBOT with LIME SAUCE

Turbot de Ligne en Tronçons Rôti sur l'Arête, Jus Acidulé

4 SERVINGS

5 tablespoons clarified butter (see note, page 53)
1 turbot head or 1 pound fish bones
5 shallots, chopped
1 celery stalk, chopped
2 scallions, chopped
¼ red bell pepper, diced
1 garlic clove, minced
½ pound chestnuts
4 turbot steaks, about 6 ounces each
(see note below)
Salt and freshly ground black pepper to taste

3 tablespoons salted butter
1 tablespoon extra virgin olive oil

LIME SAUCE:
3 tablespoons rice wine vinegar
1 teaspoon muscovado sugar
(or dark brown sugar)
½ teaspoon paprika
1 teaspoon freshly ground Szechuan pepper
Zest of 1 lime
4 cup extra virgin olive oil

Preheat the oven to 375 degrees. Heat the clarified butter in a large saucepan. Add the fish head or bones, shallots, celery, scallions, red pepper, and garlic. Sauté over high heat for 5 minutes, until golden. Add enough water just to cover and simmer for 1 hour. Strain and set aside.

Slash the chestnut shells with a sharp knife. Place on a baking sheet and roast for about 20 minutes, until the shells split open and the meat is soft but not mushy and brown. Remove from the oven and cool for a few minutes. When cool enough to handle, peel the chestnuts and set aside.

Season the turbot steaks with salt and pepper and place in a roasting pan. Scatter the chestnuts around them and drizzle with olive oil. Dot with the salted butter and roast for 15 minutes.

Meanwhile, prepare the lime sauce: combine the rice wine vinegar, muscovado sugar, paprika, Szechuan pepper, and lime zest in a saucepan. Simmer over medium heat until the vinegar has almost disappeared. Add the fish stock and reduce to ⅓ cup. Whisk in the olive oil. Arrange the turbot and chestnuts on a serving platter and serve the sauce on the side.

NOTE: Turbot is a mild white fish that can be found in better fish markets. If not available, substitute with halibut or striped bass.

TUNA STEAK with FRESH HERBS and CLAMS

Thon Rouge de Méditerranée aux Herbes Fraîches et Palourdes

4 SERVINGS

10 plum tomatoes
½ cup extra virgin olive oil
1 red bell pepper
¾ pound littleneck clams
¼ cup elderflower vinegar or Champagne vinegar
2 tablespoons muscovado sugar (or dark brown sugar)
4 tuna steaks, about 6 ounces each (preferably bluefin tuna)

Salt and freshly ground black pepper to taste

HERB PISTOU:
1 cup packed basil leaves
1 cup packed Italian parsley leaves
1 cup packed fresh coriander leaves
1 garlic clove
Salt and freshly ground black pepper to taste
¾ cup extra virgin olive oil

Preheat the oven to 400 degrees. Halve the tomatoes and discard the seeds. Place on a baking sheet. Drizzle with 2 tablespoons of olive oil and roast for 20 minutes. Set aside. Place the pepper in the oven and roast for 5 to 10 minutes, until the skin is charred and blistered. Place in a paper bag to cool.

To make the herb pistou: place the herbs, garlic, salt, and pepper in a large wood or marble mortar. Pound with the pestle until the mixture becomes a paste. While pounding and mixing, slowly add the olive oil until the mixture is thick and emulsified. Set aside.

Thoroughly rinse the clams to remove any sand. Heat 3 tablespoons of olive oil in a large saucepan. Add the clams, cover, and cook for 2 to 3 minutes or until just open. Remove the clams from their shells and add to the herb pistou.

Combine the vinegar and sugar in a small saucepan and reduce by half. Set aside. Peel and seed the roasted pepper, cut into strips, and combine with the roasted tomatoes.

Heat the remaining olive oil in a large skillet over medium-high heat. Season the tuna steaks with salt and pepper on both sides. Cook for 3 minutes on each side, making sure not to overcook the tuna.

Spoon and spread some herb pistou over the bottom of four individual serving plates. Slice the tuna steaks and arrange on top of the sauce. Garnish with the tomatoes and peppers and drizzle with some of the vinegar syrup.

MEATS

CHICKEN with
PORCINI

SQUAB with FRESH
ALMOND MILK

ROASTED MALLARD DUCK
with FIGS

DUCK with GREEN AND BLACK
OLIVES

FILET MIGNON à la
PROVENÇALE

RACK of LAMB EN CROÛTE

LAMB LOINS with TOMATOES

CHICKEN with PORCINI
Poularde aux Cèpes

2 SERVINGS

4 quarts chicken stock
1 small organic chicken, about 3 pounds
1 pound fresh porcini mushrooms
8 tablespoons unsalted butter

½ cup crème fraîche
1 large shallot, minced
Salt and freshly ground black pepper to taste
2 tablespoons minced chives

Bring the chicken stock to a boil in a large stockpot. Lightly season with salt. Truss the chicken and add it to the stock. Lower the heat to simmer and poach for 30 minutes. Remove the chicken from the broth and set aside.

Meanwhile, clean the porcini and separate the caps from the stalks. Cut the stalks into big chunks.

Heat 4 tablespoons of butter in a large skillet and sauté the porcini caps for 5 to 10 minutes, until all of the moisture is released. Remove the caps from the skillet and set aside.

Add the mushroom juices to the chicken stock along with the stalks. Reduce the chicken stock over high heat to 3 cups. Add the crème fraîche and reduce briefly until the sauce is silky but not thick.

Heat the remaining butter in a clean skillet and sauté the reserved porcini for 10 to 15 minutes, until soft and dark brown. Stir in the shallot and cook for 2 minutes. Add to the sauce.

Carve the chicken into serving pieces and add them to the sauce. Adjust the seasoning with salt and pepper to taste and simmer for 10 minutes. Sprinkle with chives just before serving.

SQUAB with FRESH ALMOND MILK
Pigeon au Lait d'Amandes Fraîches

4 SERVINGS

2 large yellow bell peppers

2 large red bell peppers

7 tablespoons extra virgin olive oil

6 roasted piquillo peppers (see note below)

1 large red onion, thinly sliced

2 teaspoons honey

¼ teaspoon paprika

Salt and freshly ground black pepper to taste

3 ounces shelled fresh almonds or blanched almonds

1 cup crème fraîche

4 squab, about 15 ounces each

2 shallots, minced

½ cup Madeira wine or sweet dessert wine

2 cups chicken stock

Juice of half a grapefruit

¼ teaspoon ground mace

2 tablespoons unsalted butter

1 garlic clove, minced

2 cups packed baby spinach

Preheat the oven to 450 degrees. Rub the red and yellow peppers with 2 table-spoons of the olive oil and place on a baking sheet. Roast for 8 minutes on each side, until they are charred and blistered. Remove from the oven and place in a paper bag to cool. When cool enough to handle, remove the skin and discard the seeds and core. Cut the red, yellow, and piquillo peppers into ½-inch strips.

Heat 2 tablespoons olive oil in a large skillet over medium heat. Add the onion slices, and cook until translucent but not brown. Stir in the honey, pa-prika, and the peppers. Cook for 1 minute. Season with salt and pepper to taste.

To make the almond milk, combine the almonds and crème fraîche in a small saucepan and simmer for 10 minutes. Remove from the heat and set aside to infuse for 10 minutes. Puree the mixture in a food processor, return to the pan, and simmer for 2 minutes. Strain and set aside.

Rinse and dry the squab. Season with salt and pepper inside and outside. Rub with 2 tablespoons of olive oil and place in a roasting pan. Place in the oven and roast at 450 degrees for 20 minutes. The squab should be medium rare. Carve the legs and breasts from the squab and keep warm. Lightly crush the carcasses.

Heat the remaining 1 tablespoon of olive oil in a deep skillet and sauté the shallots with the carcasses until golden. Deglaze with the wine and reduce by half. Add the chicken stock, grapefruit juice, and mace. Reduce the sauce by half. Strain through a fine-meshed strainer. Adjust seasoning with salt and pepper to taste and whisk in 1 tablespoon of butter until emulsified. Keep warm.

Meanwhile, heat the remaining 1 tablespoon of butter in a skillet until hazelnut color. Toss in the garlic and spinach and cook until just wilted. Reheat the peppers and the almond milk. To serve, spoon the peppers onto 4 serving plates. Top with the squab legs and breasts and place the spinach on the side. Drizzle with the squab sauce and almond milk.

NOTE: Piquillo peppers are grown only in the Navarre region of Spain. They are available, roasted and peeled, in jars in gourmet shops.

ROASTED MALLARD DUCK with FIGS

Canard Colvert Rôti aux Figues

2 SERVINGS

1 mallard duck, about 2½ pounds (see note)

4 tablespoons unsalted butter

1 carrot, diced

1 onion, diced

1 tomato, diced

2½ cups white wine

Salt and freshly ground black pepper to taste

1 tablespoon extra virgin olive oil

6 fresh figs

1½ cups red wine, preferably Côtes du Rhône

1 small stick cinnamon

Cut off the wing tips of the duck and set aside with the neck and gizzard. Rinse the duck and dry with paper towels. To prepare the duck stock, heat 2 tablespoons of butter in a large saucepan over high heat. Add the carrot, onion, tomato, and the reserved wing tips, neck, and gizzard. Cook, stirring once in a while, for 5 minutes or until the mixture becomes golden brown. Add 2 cups of white wine along with 2 cups of water. Bring to a low simmer and cook for about 30 minutes, skimming once in a while, or until the mixture has reduced by a half. Strain through a fine sieve and reserve.

Preheat the oven to 400 degrees. Season the duck with salt and pepper inside and out and rub with olive oil. Roast for 30 to 40 minutes. The duck should be medium rare. Meanwhile, peel the figs, leaving them whole.

Reserve the skins. Combine the red wine and cinnamon in a saucepan large enough to hold the figs in a single layer. Add the figs and poach over medium-low heat for 15 minutes. Remove the figs and keep warm. Reduce the poaching liquid by half.

Remove the duck from the roasting pan and keep warm. Pour off and discard fat from pan. Deglaze with the remaining ½ cup of white wine. Add the reserved fig skins and the reduced poaching liquid. Adjust seasoning with salt and pepper to taste and strain.

Carve the duck into serving pieces and place in a shallow serving dish. Halve the figs and arrange around the duck pieces. Spoon the sauce over them and serve immediately.

NOTE: Mallard duck is a lean, flavorful duck available only from October through February. Mallard ducks are available at www.dartagnan.com.

SAVEURS DE PROVENCE: Figs

The fig tree is deeply rooted in the history of Provence. Over the years, all sorts of beliefs and superstitions have been associated with its fruit. It has been seen both as a symbol of fertility and as a demonic object. Because the tree loses its leaves, an unusual phenomenon in Mediterranean regions, it is also a rare indicator of the seasons.

Fresh figs are available here from mid-June to December and accessible to all. But once dried the fruits can be eaten throughout the year anywhere in the world. The drying process is both the simplest and the best way to preserve figs. In Provence, they are traditionally dried in the sun on stone terraces, and then stored in metal containers layered with laurel leaves. Figs go well with cantaloupe, ham, and strong cheeses such as goat or Roquefort.

DUCK with GREEN and BLACK OLIVES

Canard aux Olives

4 SERVINGS

1 duck, about 5 pounds
5 ounces green olives
5 ounces black olives
4 tablespoons unsalted butter
2 carrots, diced
1 onion, diced
1 shallot, diced

1 garlic clove, chopped
1 leek, cut into thin slices
1 celery stalk, thinly sliced
2 cups white wine
Salt and freshly ground black pepper to taste
2 cups Madeira wine

Cut the wing tips off the duck and reserve. Set aside the liver and add the neck and gizzard to the wing tips. Rinse the duck and dry with paper towels. Chop the liver and reserve.

Pit the green and black olives and reserve the pits. Blanch the green olives in boiling water for 5 minutes and drain.

To prepare the duck stock: heat 2 tablespoons of butter in a large saucepan over high heat. Add carrots, onion, shallot, garlic, leek, celery, and the reserved wing tips, neck, and gizzard. Cook, stirring once in a while, for 5 minutes or until the mixture becomes golden brown. Add the white wine along with 2 cups of water. Bring to a low simmer and cook for about 30 minutes, skimming once in a while, or until the mixture has reduced by half. Strain through a fine sieve. Reserve.

Preheat the oven to 425 degrees. Season the duck with salt and pepper inside and out. Roast the duck for 30 minutes. Lower the heat to 350 and continue to roast for about an hour. Meanwhile, combine the Madeira wine and the olive pits in a saucepan, and reduce by half over medium heat. Add the reserved duck stock and reduce by half.

Stir in the chopped reserved liver and cook
until the sauce thickens. Add salt and pepper to
taste, and strain though a fine sieve into a clean
saucepan. Whisk in the remaining butter over low heat to
emulsify the sauce. Add the black and green olives and cook briefly
until the olives are hot.

Carve the duck into serving pieces and place in a shallow
serving dish. Spoon the sauce over it.

SAVEURS DE PROVENCE: Garlic

Centuries ago, garlic spread across Europe and Asia from the plains of the Caspian Sea. Traditionally, garlic has been valued for its numerous non-culinary qualities, notably its use in combating illness. During plague epidemics, it was valued as one of the few remedies available. In the past, newlyweds were served garlic soup on the morning after their nuptial night. The potent herb was considered an aphrodisiac and a tonic to boost their fertility.

Garlic grows easily in Provence, where the mild winters allow it to be planted in the fall and harvested during the summer months. It is essential to Mediterranean cuisine; any dish called "à la Provençale" must contain the triumvirate of garlic, tomatoes, and olive oil. Until recently, a lunch in Provence always included garlic-rubbed bread slices drizzled with olive oil. Other characteristic dishes that make use of this pungent bulb are crushed tomatoes, leg of lamb studded with garlic, bouillabaisse, and aïoli (a garlic mayonnaise made with olive oil and served with fish or snails). Aïoli is so prevalent in Provence that it merits its own festival called "Le Grand Aïoli," a celebration featuring a grand feast of vegetables alongside the garlic-rich spread.

FILET MIGNON à la PROVENÇALE

Filet de Boeuf à la Provençale

4 SERVINGS

4 tablespoons unsalted butter

3 shallots, minced

1 bottle good-quality red wine

1 sprig thyme

1 bay leaf

2 garlic cloves, chopped

1 tablespoon Sarawak or any black
peppercorns, crushed

1½ cups beef stock

Salt and freshly ground black pepper to taste

2 medium eggplants

2 tablespoons extra virgin olive oil

2 large tomatoes, peeled, seeded, and quartered
(see note, page 36)

1 large mild onion, thinly sliced

1 large red bell pepper, thinly sliced

½ teaspoon sugar

½ pound baby pattypan squash

4 beef filets mignons, about 7 ounces each

Heat 1 tablespoon of butter in a saucepan over medium heat. Add the shallots and cook until translucent but not brown. Add the red wine, thyme, bay leaf, garlic, and peppercorns. Reduce to ½ cup over medium-high heat. Add the beef stock and reduce until the sauce is syrupy. Adjust seasoning to taste with salt. Reserve.

Preheat the oven to 450 degrees. Split the eggplants lengthwise, season with salt and pepper, and rub with 1 tablespoon of olive oil. Place on a baking sheet and roast for 15 minutes, until soft. Scoop out the flesh and puree in a food processor until smooth. Adjust seasoning with salt and pepper and set aside.

Heat the remaining 1 tablespoon of olive oil in a skillet over medium heat. Add the onion and pepper slices and cook until soft but not brown. Add the tomatoes, season with salt, pepper, and sugar, and simmer until all liquid has evaporated and the mixture is dry.

Steam the pattypan squash over salted water until cooked through but still firm and crisp. Heat the remaining 3 tablespoons butter in a skillet over medium-high heat. Season the filets with salt and pepper on both sides. Cook for 4 minutes on each side for medium-rare, or longer according to taste. Remove from the skillet and let the meat rest for 5 minutes.

Reheat the sauce over low heat. To serve, spread some of the pepper and tomato mixture in the center of four serving plates. Top each with a filet mignon and arrange the pattypan squashes and eggplant puree around. Spoon some of the sauce over and serve immediately.

RACK of LAMB EN CROÛTE

Canon d'Agneau en Croûte

4 TO 5 SERVINGS

2 racks of lamb, 8 ribs each

4 tablespoons extra virgin olive oil

1 carrot, diced

1 onion, diced

1 leek, thinly sliced

2 cups white wine

1 tomato, diced

3 sprigs thyme

2 tablespoons unsalted butter

1 pound white mushrooms, minced

1 shallot, minced

Juice of half a lemon

Salt and freshly ground black pepper to taste

1 pound good-quality store-bought puff pastry

½ cup store-bought tapenade (see note)

1 egg yolk, beaten

Have your butcher bone the racks of lamb by carefully removing the loins in one piece. Reserve the bones. To make the lamb sauce: heat 2 tablespoons of olive oil in a deep skillet over high heat. Add the lamb bones and sauté until deep brown on all sides. Stir in the carrot, onion, and leek and cook until golden brown. Add the white wine and scrape the bottom of the pan with a wooden spatula to release the cooking bits. Add 2 cups of water and reduce slightly. Add the diced tomato, lower the heat to medium, and reduce by half. Strain into a saucepan. Add the sprigs of thyme and reserve.

Heat the butter in a large skillet over medium heat. Toss in the mushrooms, shallots, lemon juice, salt, and pepper. Cook, stirring constantly, until all liquid has evaporated and the mixture is dry. Set aside to cool.

Season the lamb loins with salt and pepper. Heat the remaining 2 tablespoons olive oil in a large skillet over medium-high heat. Sear the lamb loins for 1 minute on all sides for rare and a minute or two longer for medium rare. Remove from the skillet and cool.

Preheat the oven to 450 degrees. Roll out the puff pastry into a rectangle about 12-inch by 8-inch and ⅛-inch thick. Halve the dough into two equal pieces.

Divide the mushroom mixture and spread evenly on each rectangle. Top each with ¼ cup of tapenade followed by a lamb loin. Fold the dough over, pressing down around the edges to seal. Brush the top with the egg. Place on a baking sheet and bake for 10 minutes, until the pastry is golden.

Reheat the lamb sauce over medium heat. Discard the thyme sprigs. Cut the lamb into serving slices and serve with the lamb sauce on the side.

NOTE: Tapenade is a black or green olive puree flavored with herbs and anchovies. It is available in most gourmet stores.

LAMB LOINS with TOMATOES

Emincés d'Agneau à la Tomate

4 SERVINGS

5 small tomatoes, 1 reserved whole and
4 peeled (see note, page 36)
½ cup extra virgin olive oil
2 racks of lamb, 8 ribs each
1 carrot, diced
1 onion, diced
1 leek, thinly sliced
2 cups white wine
1 zucchini, thinly sliced
1 medium eggplant, thinly sliced
Salt and freshly ground black pepper
to taste
2 tablespoons unsalted butter
1 pound spinach, stemmed

BÉARNAISE SAUCE:

2 shallots, minced
3 tablespoons minced tarragon
¼ cup white wine vinegar
3 egg yolks, beaten
12 tablespoons butter, clarified, at room temperature
(see note page 53)

Preheat the oven to 250 degrees. Halve the peeled tomatoes lengthwise and discard the seeds. Place the tomato halves on a baking sheet and drizzle with 2 tablespoons of olive oil. Bake for 2 hours.

Have your butcher bone the racks of lamb by carefully removing the loins in one piece. Reserve the bones and refrigerate the loins until ready to use. To make the lamb sauce: dice the remaining tomato. Heat 2 tablespoons of olive oil in a deep skillet over high heat. Add the lamb bones and sauté until deep brown on all sides. Stir in the carrot, onion, and leek and cook until golden brown. Add the white wine and scrape the bottom of the pan with a wooden spatula to release the browned bits. Add 2 cups of water and reduce slightly. Add the diced tomato, reduce the heat to low, and simmer until the liquid has reduced by half. Strain into a saucepan.

To make the béarnaise sauce, place the minced shallots, 2 tablespoons tarragon, and vinegar in a saucepan. Reduce over medium heat until all of the liquid has evaporated. Remove from the heat and cool. Add the egg yolks to the saucepan along with 1 tablespoon of cold water. Place over low heat and whisk vigorously until the mixture is creamy and smooth. Slowly add the clarified butter, whisking constantly, until thick and emulsified. Season to taste with salt and pepper. Pass the béarnaise through a fine-meshed strainer, stir in the remaining tarragon, and keep warm.

Preheat the oven to 350 degrees. Line a baking sheet with parchment paper. Arrange the zucchini and eggplant slices into rows, alternating and overlapping them. Season with salt and pepper, drizzle with 2 tablespoons of olive oil, and bake for 10 minutes, or until the vegetables are soft but hold their shape.

Heat the remaining olive oil in a large skillet over high heat. Season the lamb loins with salt and pepper. Cook the meat for 3 to 4 minutes on each side, or according to taste. Remove from the pan and keep warm.

Heat the butter in a large skillet over medium heat. When the butter turns hazelnut brown, toss in the spinach, season with salt and pepper, and cook for 2 minutes until just wilted.

To serve, cut the lamb into thin slices and arrange on serving plates. Add the spinach and a few roasted zucchini and eggplants slices. Garnish with roasted tomatoes. Spoon some of the béarnaise on top of the lamb and drizzle the lamb jus around the meat and vegetables. Serve the extra béarnaise on the side.

VEGETABLES

ARTICHOKE MOUSSE

EGGPLANT GRATIN

CRUSHED POTATOES
with CHIVES

ZUCCHINI GRATIN

CHANTERELLES and FRESH NAVY
BEANS FRICASSEE in OLIVE OIL

SAUTEED EGGPLANTS
with PARMESAN

ARTICHOKE MOUSSE

Mousseline d' Artichaut

4 SERVINGS

1 tablespoon flour
Juice of 1 lemon
16 small purple artichokes
2 cups crème fraîche
2 teaspoons unsalted butter
2 tablespoons truffle juice
Salt and freshly ground black pepper to taste

Bring a large pot of salted water to a boil. Add the flour and lemon juice and stir well to dissolve the flour.

Cut off the stems of the artichokes across the base. Break off the dark outer leaves until the pale tender ones are exposed. Using a sharp pairing knife, trim all around the bases as closely as possible without cutting or shaving the hearts. Cut crosswise, removing the top two-thirds of the leaves. Halve the artichoke hearts. Scrape out the center chokes.

Add the artichoke hearts to the lemon water and cook for 15 minutes. Drain well and puree in a food processor. Pass the mixture through a sieve, pressing down with a rubber spatula to obtain a fine, creamy puree.

Beat the crème fraîche, butter, and truffle juice into the artichoke puree. Adjust seasoning to taste with salt and pepper. Reheat, stirring constantly, and serve immediately.

EGGPLANT GRATIN

Gratin d'Aubergines

4 SERVINGS

4 medium eggplants
¾ cup plus 1 tablespoon extra virgin olive oil
¼ cup minced basil
½ cup bread crumbs

TOMATO SAUCE:

4 pounds ripe tomatoes, peeled, halved crosswise,
and seeded (see note, page 36)
4 tablespoons extra virgin olive oil

3 garlic cloves, peeled
1 onion, minced
1 tablespoon sugar
1 tablespoon tomato paste
3 sprigs parsley
1 small sprig thyme
1 bay leaf
Basil or tarragon to taste (optional)
Salt and freshly ground black pepper to taste

To make the tomato sauce: Heat the olive oil over medium-high heat in a large saucepan. Add the whole garlic cloves and cook, stirring, until golden. Add the onion, lower the heat, and cook until translucent but not brown. Add the tomatoes, sugar, tomato paste, parsley, thyme, bay leaf, and, optionally, the basil or tarragon to taste. Season with salt and pepper. Bring to a boil, lower the heat to simmer, and cook for 1 hour, stirring as needed.

Meanwhile, peel the eggplants and cut them lengthwise into ¼-inch slices. Heat ¾ cup of the olive oil in a large skillet over medium-high heat. Add a few eggplant slices to the skillet and cook until golden on both sides. Drain on paper towels. Repeat with the remaining slices.

Coat the bottom of a gratin dish with the remaining 1 tablespoon of olive oil. Spread a third of the tomato sauce in a layer. Cover with half of the eggplant slices, sprinkle with half of the minced basil. Repeat the layers finishing with a layer of tomato sauce. Sprinkle with bread crumbs.

Preheat the oven to 450 degrees. Prepare the bain-marie (hot water bath): select a roasting pan large enough to hold the gratin dish. Add several layers of paper towel at the bottom of the pan. Place the gratin dish on top and add enough boiling water to come up 1½ inches along the sides of the dish. Carefully, place the pan in the oven. Bake for 15 minutes or until hot and bubbly. Serve immediately.

NOTE: The gratin can be prepared and assembled several hours in advance and cooked just before serving.

SAVEURS DE PROVENCE:
Herbes de Provence

Provence is the most fragrant region of France, home to a variety of aromatic flowering herbs. Originally, herbs were harvested for their medicinal properties, but today they are primarily used in cooking. Herbes de Provence is a generic term for a blend of thyme, rosemary, summer savory, and oregano leaves. Serpolet, a wild creeping thyme, and marjoram, similar to oregano, are often included. Each herb brings a distinctive taste to the mix; thyme has an aroma favored by bees, while savory boasts a hot peppery flavor—and a reputation as an aphrodisiac.

The Herbes de Provence blend is traditionally dry, facilitating transportation and storage. These herbs keep their flavor long after they are dried and pair well with grilled vegetables and in game preparations, where the mix underscores the taste of the aged meat.

CRUSHED POTATOES
with CHIVES
Pommes de Terre Ecrasées à la Ciboulette

4 SERVINGS

4 medium russet potatoes
6 tablespoons unsalted butter, at room temperature
1 small bunch chives, finely minced
Coarse sea salt

Preheat the oven to 350 degrees. Wash and scrub the potatoes and dry with paper towels. Poke 8 to 12 deep holes with a fork. Place the potatoes on a baking sheet and bake for 1 hour, until they are soft.

Meanwhile, place the butter and chives in a food processor and blend thoroughly. Press the mixture through a fine strainer, scraping and pushing with a rubber spatula. The butter should be green. Chill until ready to use.

Remove the potatoes from the oven and cool slightly. Preheat the broiler. When cool enough to handle, peel and place the potatoes in a baking dish. Crush lightly each one with the tines of a fork. Scatter a few pieces of the chive butter on top and place under the broiler for a couple of minutes, until the butter is melted.

Crush with a fork to the consistency of a coarse puree. Sprinkle with sea salt and serve immediately.

Basilic

ZUCCHINI GRATIN

Gratin de Courgettes

4 SERVINGS

4 medium zucchini
¼ pound white mushrooms
4 tablespoons unsalted butter
Salt and freshly ground black pepper to taste
10 sprigs chive, minced
4 sprigs parsley, minced
1½ cups crème fraîche

Peel and cut the zucchini crosswise into ¼-inch slices. Clean and trim the white mushrooms and finely slice them. Bring a pot of salted water to a boil. Blanch the zucchini slices for 2 minutes. Drain and pat dry with paper towels.

Heat 2 tablespoons of the butter in a skillet over medium heat. Sauté the zucchini slices until just golden. Remove from the heat and season with salt and pepper to taste. Toss in the chives and parsley.

Heat the remaining butter in a skillet and sauté the mushroom slices until golden and all liquid has evaporated. Season with salt and pepper to taste.

Pour the crème fraîche in a flame-proof gratin dish, place over medium heat, and reduce until lightly thickened. Layer a third of the zucchini slices into the gratin dish. Cover with half of the mushrooms slices. Repeat the layers with the remaining ingredients. Press down with a fork to immerse all the ingredients in the cream.

Preheat the oven to 400 degrees. Prepare the bain-marie (hot water bath): select a roasting pan large enough to hold the gratin dish. Add several layers of paper towel at the bottom of the pan. Place the gratin dish on top and add enough boiling water to come up 1½ inches along the sides of the dish. Carefully, place the pan in the oven. Cook for 10 minutes or until hot and bubbly. Serve immediately.

CHANTERELLES and FRESH NAVY BEANS FRICASSEE in OLIVE OIL

Fricassée de Girolles et Coco Frais à l'Huile d'Olive

4 SERVINGS

1 pound fresh chanterelles
½ pound fresh navy beans or cranberry beans, shelled
Salt and freshly ground black pepper
2 cups chicken broth
1 tablespoon olive oil
1 tablespoon chervil leaves
1 tablespoon minced chives
1 shallot, minced

Clean the chanterelles and trim off the stems. Halve the mushrooms lengthwise and rinse under cold running water. Drain on kitchen towels.

Simmer the fresh beans in lightly salted chicken broth for 15 minutes. Remove from the heat and cool the beans in the broth.

When ready to serve, drain the beans. Heat the olive oil in a large skillet over high heat. Sauté the chanterelles until lightly golden. Toss in the beans and cook until just warm. Season to taste with salt and pepper and stir in the chervil, chives, and shallot. Serve immediately.

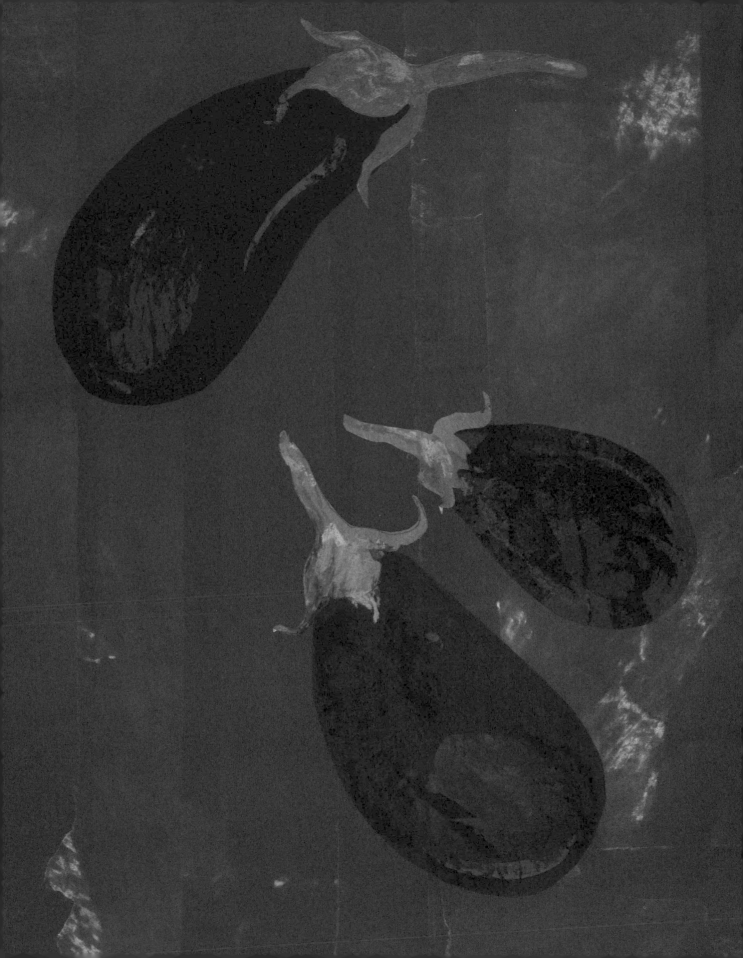

SAUTEED EGGPLANTS
with PARMESAN
Aubergines Poelées au Parmesan

4 SERVINGS

3 medium eggplants
½ cup extra virgin olive oil
Salt and freshly ground black pepper to taste
1 cup grated Parmesan cheese
¼ cup chopped Italian parsley
2 scallions, minced

Cut the eggplants crosswise into ¾-inch slices. Divide the olive oil between two large skillets and heat over medium-high heat. Add the eggplant slices in one layer to the skillets and lower the heat to medium. Cook until the slices are golden on both sides and soft. Season with salt and pepper.

Sprinkle the slices with the Parmesan. Carefully, flip them over, cheese side down, to allow the cheese to melt and form a golden crust.

Arrange the slices, cheese side up, on a serving platter. Sprinkle with the parsley and scallions and serve immediately.

DESSERTS

APRICOT SOUFFLE

STRAWBERRY GAZPACHO with
OLIVE OIL ICE CREAM

CHOCOLATE with FRESH BERRIES

SPICED PEAR TARTLET

RED BERRIES MARINATED in
MELON with RASPBERRY SORBET

ALMOND SOUP

BASIL AND STRAWBERRIES
with LEMON MOUSSE

GOAT CHEESE WAFER CAKE with
BLACK CURRANTS

APRICOT SOUFFLE

Soufflé Chaud à l'Abricot

4 SERVINGS

2 cups milk
1 vanilla bean, split
4 eggs, separated
¼ cup plus 3 tablespoons sugar,
plus extra for the soufflé molds
½ cup flour
2 teaspoons unsalted butter, softened

1 egg white
2 apricots, diced

PUREED APRICOTS:
1 pound apricots
1 cup sugar
Juice of 1 lemon

To prepare the pureed apricots: halve the apricots and discard the stones. Cut each half into ¼-inch cubes. Combine the sugar with 2 cups of water and the lemon juice in a heavy saucepan. Bring to a boil and add the apricots. Lower the heat to simmer and poach for 20 minutes. Remove from the heat and cool. Puree the mixture in a food processor.

To prepare the pastry cream, combine the milk with the vanilla bean and bring just to a boil over medium-low heat. Remove from the heat and set aside. Combine the egg yolks and ¼ cup of the sugar in a mixing bowl. Whisk until the mixture is thick and pale yellow. Fold in the flour.

Remove the vanilla bean from the milk. Slowly whisk ½ cup of hot milk into the egg and flour mixture, until smooth and well combined. Stir the mixture into the remaining hot milk and return the saucepan to medium-low heat. Cook, whisking constantly, until the mixture thickens. Lower the heat and cook for 2 to 3 minutes, stirring constantly. Remove from the heat and stir in 1 cup of the pureed apricots. Set aside to cool.

Preheat the oven to 425 degrees. Lightly butter four individual soufflé molds. Sprinkle with sugar and rotate molds to coat the bottom and sides. Gently tap the molds upside down to remove excess sugar.

Place the 5 egg whites in the bowl of an electric mixer and beat until soft peaks form. Add the 3 tablespoons of sugar and beat until stiff and shiny. Fold into the pastry cream with a rubber spatula until well combined. Fill the soufflé molds halfway with the batter. Add a little diced uncooked apricot to each mold and cover with the remaining batter.

Bake for 10 minutes, or until the soufflés have risen and are golden on top. Serve immediately with the remaining pureed apricots on the side.

STRAWBERRY GAZPACHO with OLIVE OIL ICE CREAM

Gaspacho de Fraises Citronnées avec Glace à l'Huile d'Olive

4 TO 5 SERVINGS

¼ cup sugar
2 red bell peppers, thinly sliced
1 pound strawberries, hulled
½ cup lemon juice

OLIVE OIL ICE CREAM:
1 cup milk
1 cup heavy cream
3 egg yolks
¼ cup sugar
¼ cup extra virgin olive oil

Combine the sugar with 1 cup of water in a saucepan. Bring to a boil and cook for 2 minutes until the sugar is dissolved. Add the red pepper strips to the hot syrup and set aside to infuse for 15 minutes.

To make the olive oil ice cream, combine the milk and cream in a saucepan and bring just to a boil. Remove from the heat.

Place the egg yolks and sugar in a mixing bowl. Whisk together until the mixture is light, fluffy, and pale yellow. Whisk in the olive oil. Slowly add the cream and milk mixture, whisking constantly. Return the mixture to the heat and simmer, stirring constantly, until the mixture is thick and registers 180 degrees on a candy thermometer. Set aside to cool.

Pour the cooled custard into the bowl of an ice cream maker, and churn for about 10 minutes or to creamy consistency.

Place the strawberries and lemon juice in the bowl of a food processor or blender and puree. Pour into a bowl and stir in the infused red pepper and 1 cup of the syrup. Serve in shallow serving plates topped with a scoop of olive oil ice cream.

CHOCOLATE with FRESH BERRIES

Plié au Chocolat aux Fruits

6 SERVINGS

1 cup raspberries, plus some for garnish
1 cup strawberries, plus some for garnish
2 tablespoons sugar
2 tablespoons Grand Marnier
1 cup heavy cream
8 ounces dark chocolate couverture
(available in specialty baking shops)
8 tablespoons unsalted butter

1 small orange, cut into thin wedges
1 small peach, cut into thin wedges

CRÈME PÂTISSIÈRE:
2 cups milk
5 egg yolks
¼ cup sugar
½ cup flour

To make the berry coulis, cut the raspberries and strawberries into small dice. Combine ⅓ cup of water with the 2 tablespoons of sugar. Bring to a boil and cook for 2 minutes. Remove from the heat, and stir in the Grand Marnier and the diced berries. Set aside to cool.

To make the crème pâtissière: Bring the milk just to a boil. Remove from the heat. Combine the egg yolks and sugar in a mixing bowl. Whisk until the mixture is thick and pale yellow. Fold in the flour. Slowly whisk in ½ cup of hot milk until smooth and well combined. Stir the mixture into the remaining hot milk and return the saucepan to medium-low heat. Cook, whisking constantly, until the mixture thickens. Lower the heat and cook for 2 to 3 minutes, stirring constantly. Set aside to cool.

Beat the heavy cream to stiff peaks and fold into the cooled crème pâtissière. Refrigerate until ready to use.

Melt the chocolate couverture and butter in a double boiler or in a small bowl set over simmering water. Stir well to combine. Spread the mixture to a thickness of about 1/16 inch onto a large chilled pastry marble and place in the refrigerator for 24 hours to chill.

While it is still pliable, cut the chocolate sheet into 7-inch circles. Spoon some of the crème pâtissière on one half circle and garnish with few slices of orange and peach. Carefully fold the chocolate over the mixture and fold into a wedge.

Carefully, transfer chocolate wedges to serving plates. Drizzle the berry coulis around each chocolate wedge and garnish with remaining peach and orange wedges, and berries.

SPICED PEAR TARTLET

Tartelettes aux Poires et aux Epices

10 TARTLETS

3 cups sugar
½ vanilla bean
¼ teaspoon ground nutmeg
3 cloves
2 tablespoons ground ginger
1 stick cinnamon
1 large piece of lemon zest
5 ripe pears, such as Bartlett
¾ cup chocolate-hazelnut spread, such as Nutella
¼ cup confectioners' sugar

PASTRY DOUGH:
12 tablespoons unsalted butter, softened, plus extra for molds
1 cup sugar
½ teaspoon salt
4 ounces ground hazelnuts
1 teaspoon vanilla extract
2 eggs
2⅔ cups flour

To make the spiced syrup: combine 1 quart of water with 2 cups of sugar in a large saucepan. Split the vanilla bean lengthwise, scrape off the seeds, and add the pod and seeds to the pan along with the spices and lemon zest. Bring to a boil and lower the heat to a simmer. Caramelize the remaining 1 cup sugar by cooking in a heavy saucepan over medium heat until it is liquid and slightly amber. Pour the caramel into the spiced syrup.

Peel the pears and remove the cores through the base using a sharp paring knife or apple corer. Immerse the pears in the syrup, bring back to a simmer and cook for about 15 minutes or until cooked through but firm. Turn off the heat and let the pears cool in the syrup.

To prepare the dough: cream the butter and sugar with a mixer until light and fluffy. Add the salt, ground hazelnuts, vanilla extract, and eggs and blend well. Add the flour at once and mix until the dough starts to come together. Do not overblend. Knead lightly on a floured work surface for 2 minutes. Wrap the dough in plastic wrap and chill for 1 hour.

Preheat the oven to 350 degrees. Lightly butter ten 4-inch individual tartlet molds. Divide the dough in half and roll out each half into a circle about ⅛-inch thick. Cut out ten circles, using a 5-inch cookie cutter. Line the prepared molds with the dough. Line the dough with parchment paper and fill with pie weights or dry beans. Bake ten minutes, remove parchment paper and weights, and bake the shells 5 minutes longer. Cool the tart shells and unmold.

When ready to serve, preheat the broiler. Coat the bottom of each tart shell with some chocolate-hazelnut spread. Halve the pears lengthwise and cut each half into ¼-inch slices, leaving them attached at the tip. Fan the pears into the tartlets and sprinkle with the confectioners' sugar. Place under the broiler until just caramelized. Serve immediately.

RED BERRIES MARINATED in MELON with RASPBERRY SORBET

Marinade de Melon aux Fruits Rouges et Sorbet Framboises

4 SERVINGS

1⅓ ounces fresh ginger, peeled
¼ cup plus ⅓ cup sugar
1 ripe Cavaillon melon or ½ cantaloupe
Juice of 1 lemon
1 pint strawberries, hulled
1 pint wild strawberries, hulled

RASPBERRY SORBET:

1 pound raspberries
½ cup sugar
Juice of 1 lemon

Place the ginger in a small saucepan and cover with cold water. Bring to a boil and drain. Repeat twice. Cut the ginger into small dice.

Combine ¼ cup sugar with 1 cup of water in a saucepan. Bring to a boil and cook for 2 minutes until the sugar is dissolved. Add the diced ginger and simmer for 5 minutes. Remove from the syrup with a slotted spoon and set aside.

Peel and seed the melon. Place in the bowl of a food processor along with the lemon juice and remaining ⅓ cup sugar. Puree until smooth. Transfer the mixture to a bowl and stir in the ginger. Refrigerate until ready to serve.

To make the sorbet, puree the raspberries with the sugar and lemon juice. Dilute with ¼ cup of water. Strain the mixture through a fine meshed strainer.

Pour the mixture into the bowl of an ice cream maker, and churn for about 10 minutes or to creamy consistency.

To serve, combine the strawberries and divide between four shallow serving dishes. Spoon some melon puree over them and top with a scoop of sorbet.

SAVEURS DE PROVENCE: Lavender

Every June, the chalky highlands of Haute Provence take on the violet-blue color of lavender, a plant with deep ties to the aesthetic heritage of the region. Lavender has been growing in Provence for centuries, though for the longest time, only bees had a use for it. Eventually pharmacists and apothecaries began selling dried lavender. At the end of the nineteenth century, lavender was distilled to extract its essence. The cultivation of lavender began in earnest around 1920; at that time, almost all lavender essence came from wild flowers. Only a few years later, most production came from cultivated plants like lavandin, a resistant hybrid that can produce 3 to 10 times more essence than wild varieties.

Today, though lavender is widely used in the cosmetics industry, its use in gastronomy is limited. Lavender honey, almost white with a strong bouquet, remains the primary food product derived from lavender. There are a few typically Provençal recipes that include the honey, including pastries, lavender-flavored chocolates, and ice creams.

ALMOND SOUP

Soupe d'Amandes

6 TO 8 SERVINGS

1 pound blanched almonds
1 cup sugar
1 quart heavy cream
2 cups milk
4 drops almond extract

DRAGÉES ICE CREAM:

1 quart milk
2 cups heavy cream
10 egg yolks
1¼ cups sugar
1 pound dragées, crushed (see note)

Place the blanched almonds in the bowl of a food processor and grind to a fine texture. Do not overprocess, it will become a paste.

Place half of the ground almonds, the sugar, heavy cream, milk, and almond extract along with ¾ cup of water in a heavy saucepan. Bring to a boil. Lower the heat to simmer and cook for 10 minutes. Strain the mixture through a fine-mesh strainer and set aside to cool. Refrigerate until ready to serve.

To make the dragées ice cream, combine the milk and cream in a saucepan and bring just to a boil. Remove from the heat.

Place the egg yolks and sugar in a mixing bowl. Whisk together until the mixture is light, fluffy, and pale yellow. Slowly add the cream and milk mixture, whisking constantly. Return the mixture to the heat, and simmer, stirring constantly, until the mixture is thick and registers 180 degrees on a candy thermometer. Stir in the remaining ground almonds and the crushed dragées. Set aside to cool.

Pour the cooled custard into the bowl of an ice cream maker, and churn for about 10 minutes or to a creamy consistency.

To serve, ladle some of the chilled almond soup into shallow serving bowls and place a scoop of ice cream in the center.

NOTE: Dragées are sugar-coated almonds available in specialty candy stores.

BASIL AND STRAWBERRIES
with LEMON MOUSSE

Basilic and Guariguettes en Citronnade Accompagnés de leurs Compotes Parfumées

BASIL COOKIE DOUGH:

2 cups flour

¼ cup sugar

12 tablespoons unsalted butter, cold and cut into small pieces

3 tablespoons minced basil leaves

1 egg, beaten

MOUSSE:

1 cup sugar

1 teaspoon gelatin

¾ cup tepid water

2 tablespoons thinly sliced basil leaves

Grated zest of 1 lemon

Juice of 2 large lemons or 3 medium

4 cups heavy cream

THREE STRAWBERRY COMPOTES:

¾ cup sugar

1 teaspoon black peppercorns

2 teaspoons fresh thyme leaves

2 teaspoons minced rosemary leaves

1½ pounds strawberries, halved

Prepare a sugar syrup for the strawberry compotes: combine 2¼ cups of water with ¾ cup sugar in a small saucepan. Bring to a boil and cook for 2 to 3 minutes, until the sugar is dissolved. Set aside to cool.

Preheat the oven to 350 degrees. To make the cookie dough: combine the flour and sugar in a large mixing bowl. Add the butter and cut into the flour and sugar with a pastry cutter or two knives. When the mixture looks crumbly, mix in the basil. Add the egg and knead the dough until smooth and homogenous.

Roll out the dough to ⅛-inch thickness on a lightly floured surface. Cut out 3-inch circles and place on an ungreased baking sheet. Bake the cookies for 10 minutes. Remove from the oven and cool.

To make the mousse: melt ¼ cup of the sugar and the gelatin in the tepid water. Stir in the basil, lemon zest, and juice. Combine the remaining ¾ cup sugar with the cream in a chilled bowl, and whip until stiff peaks form. Make sure not to overbeat. Fold the whipped cream into the lemon and basil mixture. Chill until ready to serve.

To make the three strawberry compotes: place one-third of the cooled sugar syrup in a blender, add the peppercorns, and blend for 2 minutes. Pour into a bowl and set aside. Place half of the remaining syrup in the blender along with the thyme. Blend for 2 minutes and reserve in a separate bowl. Add the remaining syrup to the blender along with the rosemary. Blend for 2 minutes and pour into a separate bowl. Divide the strawberries among the three syrups. Crush them with a fork to a chunky compote.

To serve, spoon the lemon mousse in the center of individual serving plates and surround with the three strawberry compotes. Garnish with the basil cookies.

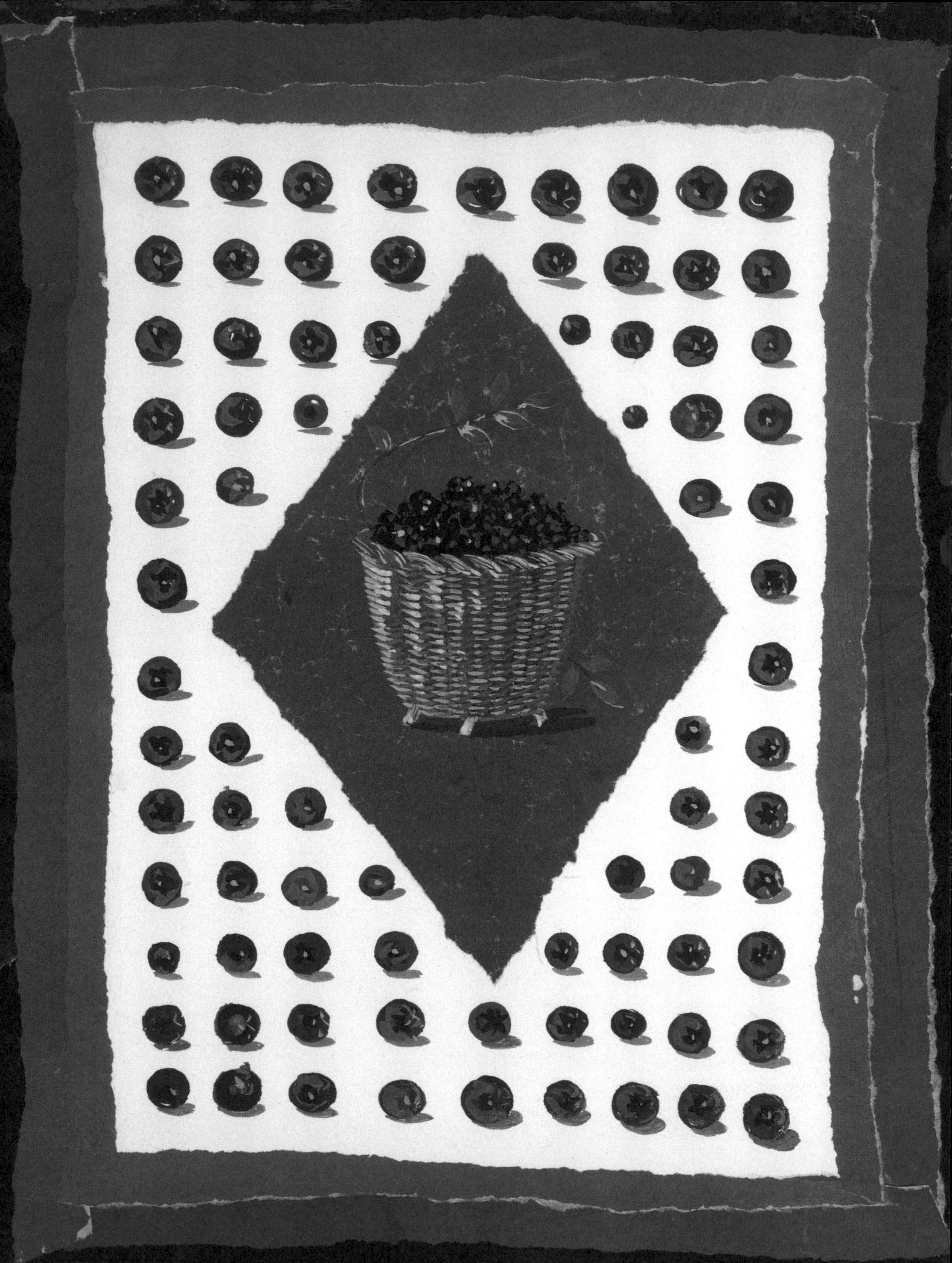

GOAT CHEESE WAFER CAKE
with BLACK CURRANTS

Croustillant de Brousse de Chèvre aux Myrtilles

8 SERVINGS

½ cup plus 2 tablespoons sugar

8 ounces fresh black currants or blueberries

8 ladyfingers

1 cup fresh goat cheese

½ cup honey

4 eggs, separated

8 egg whites

WAFERS:

½ cup sugar

2 egg whites

¼ cup flour

1 tablespoon unsalted butter, melted

2 tablespoons ground almonds

In a heavy saucepan, combine ½ cup of the sugar with 1 cup of water. Bring to a boil and cook for 2 minutes until the sugar dissolves. Add half of the black currants or blueberries and simmer for 10 minutes. Set aside to cool.

Preheat the oven to 400 degrees. Lightly butter 2 baking sheets.

To prepare the wafers, place all the ingredients into a mixing bowl. Whisk vigorously until the sugar is dissolved and the mixture is homogenous. Spoon the mixture onto one of the buttered baking sheets and spread to form 8 4-inch circles. Bake for 5 to 8 minutes, until golden. Set aside to cool.

Place 8 4-inch ring molds on the second baking sheet. Line the bottom of the rings with the ladyfingers, cutting them to fit when necessary.

Combine the goat cheese, honey, and 4 egg yolks in a mixing bowl. Whip the 4 egg whites until soft peaks form. Add the 2 tablespoons of sugar and whip until stiff peaks form. Do not overbeat. Fold the whites gently into the cheese mixture until well combined.

Pour the mixture into the prepared molds. Garnish on top with the remaining raw berries and bake for 10 minutes.

Drain the poached berries. Carefully slide the "soufflés" onto serving plates and remove the rings. Top with a wafer and spoon some of the poached berries around. Serve immediately.

ABOUT THE AUTHORS

JEAN-ANDRÉ CHARIAL is chef and proprietor of l'Oustau de Baumanière, one of the most prestigious dining and hotel establishments in Provence. His restaurant holds the honor of two Michelin stars, one of the highest marks of excellence in France, making his home village of Les Baux a destination for gastronomic enthusiasts from around the world.

Charial's career at Baumanière began with his grandfather, Raymond Thuilier, who opened the restaurant in 1945. Thuilier had been drawn to the gracious but rustic farmhouse dating from 1634 and located near the Val d'Enfer, the valley thought to have inspired Dante to write *The Divine Comedy*. Thuilier turned Baumanière into a world-class resort, and soon celebrities from Winston Churchill to the Queen of England were visiting to taste the famous cuisine. After training at the Waldorf-Astoria in New York, Charial joined his grandfather at the restaurant in 1970. During this period Charial also studied in the kitchens of French culinary masters Jean and Pierre Troisgros and Paul Bocuse, among others. By the 1980s Charial had taken charge of the restaurant and further developed the rooms and gardens that make up the hotel. Eventually his grandfather passed the mantle to Charial as head of the entire operation, and, working with his wife Geneviève, Charial expanded Baumanière, always taking care to preserve the standards of his forebear.

One of the cornerstones of Charial's style of cooking is a careful attention to the origins of the raw ingredients that come into his kitchen. Charial personally manages the planting and maintenance of vegetable gardens on the grounds of Baumanière, and he has even begun to experiment with making wine in association with nearby vintners. His wine cellar, renovated in 2002 at a cost of more than three million Euros, is world renowned and now holds 100,000 bottles. Charial has earned his place as one of France's premiere chefs, and he is devoted to spreading the wonders of Provençal cuisine across the globe.

ISABELLE DE BORCHGRAVE, a native of Brussels, has been visiting Provence since she was a child. While principally a painter, de Borchgrave works in other media including murals, costumes, collage, and textile design. Her work has been exhibited at the Musée des Arts Decoratifs in Paris and the Fashion Institute of Technology in New York. She has also created a number of houseware collections for fine retailers as well as *Fashion à la Mode: The Pop-Up Book of Costumes and Dresses*.

INDEX

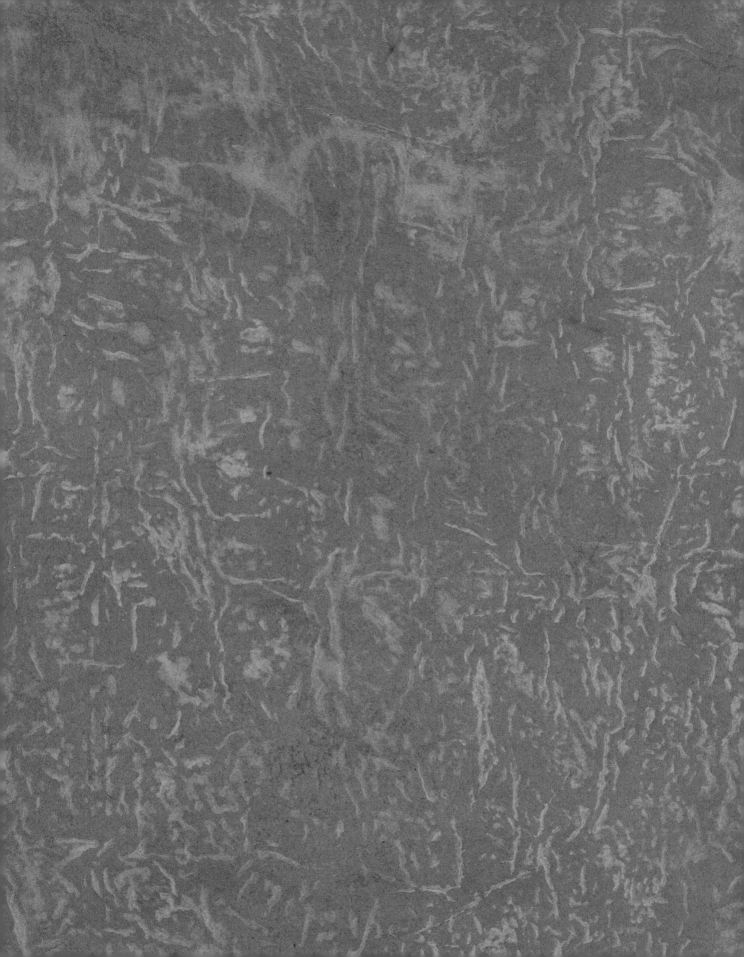